That Festive Feeling

Edited by Mark Richardson

forwardpress

First published in Great Britain in 2007 by:
Forward Press Ltd.
Remus House
Coltsfoot Drive
Peterborough
PE2 9JX
Telephone: 01733 898108
Website: www.forwardpress.co.uk

SB ISBN 978-1 84418 463 7

Foreword

Forward Press was established in 1989 to provide a platform for poets to showcase their works. Today, Forward Press continues to provide an outlet for new and established poets and *That Festive Feeling* is tribute to this.

Poetry should be interesting and, above all else, accessible to all. Forward Press publications are for all lovers of traditional verse and of the art of rhyme, as well as for those who enjoy contemporary verse. *That Festive Feeling* showcases both styles ensuring a varied read, and proving traditional and modern do complement each other.

Contents

The Poems

A Christmas Wish

Alone for Christmas
No one to love
My sons are a blessing from above
Can't find that special person
It doesn't seem to happen
Caught in the midst of in-between age
It's day by day and page to page
I've loved and lost
And lived and loved
But now it's time
I shared my wine
And found my love
At Christmas time
Let him be mine.

Chris Angel

The Spirit Of Christmas

Couple with a donkey
Husband Joseph, wife Mary
Rising shining star in the dark sky
Innkeeper offering a stable
Shepherds carrying lambs
Three wise men journey
Murmur of a baby being born
Angels above looking down
Son of God, Jesus Christ.

Martin Holmes

What I Want For Christmas

Is a drug to remind me
where I put my car keys,
a true sense of vocation,
shorter work hours, a challenging
pay rise, economic recovery,
dental checks and eye tests
free again, unpolluted,
unprivatised drinking water.

I'd like rape crisis centres to counsel men
the children who went missing
to turn up again,
a chipper lifestyle,
an endless strawberry crop,
low cholesterol chocolate soufflé.

I don't need a computer,
a trip on the Orient Express,
to be mugged by a pit bull terrier
and left by an ex-partner.
I don't need a juggernaut to plough into my lavatory,
ancillary works to carry out surgery,

a work of art that's one of a series
and looks as if it's been painted with a mop,
AIDS, a car bomb, a trip to Nova Scotia,
a cut above like a veteran mower
though I wouldn't object to an exotic
flower to surprise me at Christmas.

Rosemary Benzing

A Carol Service

A carol service in anticipation,
With the prospect of abundant Christmas cheer,
God's people made due choral preparation,
The desire for perfection very clear.
The choirmaster had some points to mention,
Having brought one more rehearsal to an end.
To him, did every member pay attention,
For he spoke to them as leader and as friend.
Much merit in the choir I am finding,
We have voice production of good quality.
But, surely, carol words are us reminding
Of our greatest need, which is sincerity.
Come with me now, to hear from the Messiah
And before the master of us, be still,
Then everyone of us will He inspire
In true harmony to sing and do His will.
Soon from their midst was driven all division,
For the former rivalry began to cease.
Throughout the choir spread the common vision,
Of the One who came to Earth as prince of peace.
Each member was transformed into God's servant,
In the carol service, all gave praise as one.
Faithful were they, most joyful and triumphant,
In the birthday celebrations of God's son.
Like herald angels, choristers were singing
And the great glad tidings did they clearly tell,
Thus serving God, as He was people bringing
To the one and only Lord Emmanuel.

D J Price

Christmas Thoughts

We won't care if the snow does snow,
We won't care if the winds do blow.
We'll be here all warm and snug
Opening parcels on the rug.

We'll be eating pudding and pie,
Perhaps a drink, sure, by and by.
But let's not forget how lucky are we
As we laugh around the Christmas tree.

For there's many a child that will see no fun,
No comfort still when the day is done.
So many a child who's living in fear
With only war noise in their ear.

So let's give thanks for how peace feels
Whilst we indulge in our Christmas meals.

Helen Langstone

My Christmas Present

I've a pressie under the tree
It was put there just for me.

It is a big red box
I wonder what's in there
I cannot wait to see.

Christmas has dawned
As I turn to the tree
To see
What's in the box for me.

With excitement and surprise
I opened my big brown eyes
To see a car waiting for me.

By the end of the day
I've discarded the car
To play with the box
What a bargain we have got.

Debbie Storey

Christmas

What are your thoughts of Christmas
Some snow or mistletoe
Or silver bells shining so bright
Maybe just a scarlet bow?
Perhaps you see a Christmas tree
With lights flashing on and off
And heaps of presents piled underneath
A fairy perched aloft.
Or do you think of snow and ice
And snowmen with eyes of coal
Some robins perching on window sills
Listening as church bells toll?
Maybe you think of that miracle birth
In that lowly distant place
When our Saviour first arrived on Earth
To save all the human race.

Elsie Sharman

Things For You

Christmas keeps on coming round every year
And instead of being filled with joy, it's filled with dreaded fear.
People sleeping by your rubbish, ransacking through your waste,
Eating the scraps of leftover food, stuffing their hungry face.

It's common to say, 'I don't believe in St Nick,'
But now it's Christmas people don't believe in, it's all become
such a trick.
Using the birth of Lord Jesus, to ask for more things
Large designer handbags, sparkly diamond rings.

Whilst others lay lonely, outside turning blue,
Watching you unwrap your presents, more things for you.
Then the endless number of relatives pour in to be fed
The poor boy on the street, doesn't know if his mother is alive or dead.

The exchanging of presents, scarves, pots, pans, planes that can fly,
A busy man throws a pound coin in an old woman's hat,
'Merry Christmas,' he mumbles as he passes by.
I don't want much for Christmas, just a nice, normal, friendly Earth
With pleases and thank yous, but people act like it's worth more
than they can afford.

But they just don't realise, courtesy doesn't cost
It just helps regain the respect our planet once lost
I just want the ozone layer, complete with no holes
I want to bring back Christmas with its attitude and soul.

I don't want to feel guilty opening presents on Christmas Day,
And boast about my brand new stuff whilst others find a warm safe
place to stay.
How can we sleep feeling fat and bloated late on Christmas night?
When seconds away is an innocent father, victim of a drunken fight.

Christmas is for rich people now, 'cause you can't celebrate it,
without any cash.
Blowing your life savings on crap that ends up in the trash.
So this year at Christmas, take time to think about what you're
going to do
Think before you write that list of extra things for you.

Think of those less fortunate and who won't be spreading cheer,
Help them learn what a smile is and how to conquer their fear.
And teach yourself to realise, what Christmas is really worth,
And maybe, if we all pitch in, we can help bring Christmas back
down to Earth.

Kendal Moran (16)

Christmas Time

Christmas time is here
Rosy cheeks and smiling tears
Loved ones all around
Captured memories in time abound
Christmases come and go
But time will always show
Loved ones will always stay
In our hearts so we pray.

Tess McHugh

Merry Lonely Christmas

The lights are on, but nobody's home
She comes home to an empty house
And drops her coat and purse,
Staring at the cold and silent room.

She's cooking just for one
But she's made too much again
As always, with no one to share,
She eats at the table alone.

Silently she clears away
And sits and stares at the blank TV
Wondering why no one cares
Why no one comes to see her.

Her tears trickle down again,
Burning trails of loneliness.
Just wondering, always wondering,
How it became this way.

Merry Christmas,
She says to herself again,
Remembering the years before
And another lonely New Year.

Kho Fung Vi

Christmas Time

It's Christmas time look at the snow
It looks like a winter wonderland
The kids are skating on the pond
Around and around as they hold hands.

It's fun to see the smiles and games
The kids are playing in the snow
They are singing and playing merrily
And they are really putting on a show.

The sleigh bells are ringing loudly
As the sleighs seem to be racing
People are waving and laughing
Those walking are frantically pacing.

It's Christmas time and you can tell
Everyone is so polite and nice
I wish it was this way all year
I'd change it now and not think twice.

On Christmas Day when kids get up
The presents are under the tree
Their eyes will seem twice the size
As they open their presents frantically.

William Lacewell Jnr

Maternity

'A Christmas baby . . . what fun!'
But my son won't think so I know
Not two celebrations - just one . . .
These last days seem terribly slow.
Tables distanced by the bump,
Steering wheel at arm's length;
As I nod off, he starts to jump,
There's no doubt at all of his strength!

Here's the first Christmas card of the year,
Joseph and Mary along Bethlehem's way;
How I pity her, poor dear,
For what awaits at the end of that day!
Not sterile maternity prepared for me,
But forced to give birth in a stable,
Animals looking sweet in pictures we see,
Are smelly and dirty, calls a Babel.

Dear Lord who survived every infant ill,
Grew to a man, knowing your fate
Death on a cross, exposed on a hill
And the three long anxious days wait.
And Mary your mother, life God dedicated,
That Messiah on Earth could be born
As prophets of old their visions related
A saviour for this world sin torn.

Jesus and Mary, as I look at that ride,
So God's Son, our world's life could share,
I pray send your angels to guard and to guide,
This baby of mine I now bear.

Di Bagshawe

I Hate Christmas!

I hate Christmas, it's such a bore
The worship of an old folklore
The thought of turkey makes me sick
And waiting up for old 'St Nick'

The shops are mad, it's very busy
This pushin' and shovin' is sending me dizzy
It's getting earlier, I swear I remember
Seeing tinsel on shelves way back in September

I really hate Christmas and all of the puds
Topping of sprouts and peeling of spuds
The kitchen which is usually mine
Is strewn with half drunk glasses of wine

The family drive me up the wall
Coats, hats and trainers are cluttering the hall
And Aunty Olive is coming again
By Boxing Day, I'll be completely insane

The doorbell is ringin'
I hear carol singin'
Surely this can't be right
Sixteen times in one night

Fools and Horses is on yet again
We were hoping for snow and yet we got rain
Hubby has skulked off to the pub
He comes home half-drunk and eats all the grub

Then we go to bed to the sound of kids' banter
Excited as they all wait up for Santa
We've left a carrot and a full glass of sherry
We hope that *our* Santa doesn't get *too merry*

On Christmas Day teatime, we all sit in a heap
Grandad is snoring and Nan's half asleep
The kids they are whinging, their toys are so boring
Dad's getting sozzled and Mom is now roarin'!

I really hate Christmas, I hate all the junk
The cheap nasty sherry that makes us all drunk
The family keep rowing
They got on my wick
The kids are now squabbling
And uncle's been sick

I truly hate Christmas, I'm glad when it's gone
Our lounge is a flea-pit, the kitchen's a bomb
When new year arrives, I will feel very smug
I really hate Christmas, bah humbug!

Julie Trainor

The Carol Singers

The snow fell fast in December
And the streets were covered
In snow
And carol singers
With all their hearts
Sang hymns that we all know

The spirit of Christmas
Was showing
As they trudged from door to door
And though they may not know it
They brought hope
To the needy and poor
And their voices
Were a message for all to hear
No matter who you are
And though the snow
Kept falling
They were not deterred
And far away in the distance
Their voices could
Still be heard.

By now the streets
Were alive once more
And people were standing
Near their door
There they gathered
The weak and the strong
And they watched in awe
As the carol singers
Moved along

And high above them
Shining bright
A heavenly star
Lit up the night.

Eddie Jepson

Christmas Crises

Christmas crucifies us all. Born premature
In October, banishing back-to-school blazers
Into dusty depths of department stores,
Scrawling its spider's web message
Across windows; summoning the bitter reflux
Of last year's excess to sear our parched throats.

Shopaholic old bags barge past bag ladies
Their Christmas crises juxtaposed. One unaware
That the switch to illuminate the empty eyes
Of her grandchildren cannot be bought; the other
Staggering between starvation and salvation.
Will there be room at the inn?

Let us return to our biblical roots.
The burning bush; Baghdad aflame;
Better had He not been born again.
Better to have been stillborn.
Second helpings? Or second coming?
Will Easter help us resurrect our self-respect?

Helen Matthews

The Sacrifice

Because it's Christmas
The pine forest is dragged into town,
Some still stand on twisted roots
Many are lying down.

The city is filled with excitement,
Pine scent exudes from the trees,
Car fumes fan the sweet branches
In place of the cool mountain breeze.

Then the plastic cocoons of green magic
Are each carried home with great care,
To be festooned with tinsel and baubles
While coloured lights shine in their hair.

Christmas is now just a memory,
The joy and the singing is past
Dead needles litter the carpets
The sweet smell of nature fades fast.

Now with the Christmas empties
They are stripped and thrown into the yard,
No one will mourn their passing
At the yearly religious charade.

S Nicolaou

Christmas Once Again

Christmas time is here again
Let's hope from it a new life we'll gain
Because it brings our Saviour back
In remembrance of which some lack
Of that wonderful day that He arrived
To a world God wanted to survive
For in God's mind there were great plans
For all humans of so many lands
To bring hope and love to everyone
A brand new era had begun
So let's remember it with great joy
That humble birth of that baby boy
Let the bells ring out loud and clear
Reminding us He's forever near.

Dolly Baldwin

All Spruced Up For Christmas

Norwegian giant
Yesterday's king of the forest
Magnificent, towering spruce
What was the use?
Reigning in a wooded world of blue and green.

An expected change of scene
Now you lie
Bleeding from the slashes of the woodman's axe
Humiliation of a king
Without a crown
Struck down
Before time
In your prime.

Roots severed, bodies stiff
Dragged away in chains
To be rehoused
Relocated to a plastic pot
Stuck in the corner of a noisy room
A haven for prettily wrapped parcels.
Coloured baubles knotted to your limp arms
Silky ribbons and trashy charms
Weigh you down
Beneath your lower limbs
Secateurs have trimmed
Away your laterals
Children crawl around you
Drooping lifeless branches,
Your needled nerves
Fall on a stained floor
Littered with Lego pieces
Raucous laughter, drunken calls
Splattered carpet, wine falls
From shaking glasses
Spoiling pretty party clothes
For you, time passes
Slowly.

Tomorrow for you another journey,
Thrown into a council skip
Dragged to a rubbish tip
Joining others high in a heap
No dignity can be kept
Take heart
Shredded into bits
Made to measure for the compost heap
And while you sleep
To live again
In time to come, mixed with earth
Rebirth
Perhaps you will bring forth a son
Who will become
Like you - a king!

Ann Wardlaw

The Meaning Of Christmas

One from afar looks in tonight,
In through the wide inviting door -
Dust from the journey stains his brow,
His shoulders droop; his feet are sore,
'Good host, my wife has got to rest,
As you can tell her time is near,
We've travelled long and now, alas
There is no room for Mary, here.'

'I'm sorry sir, I much regret . . .
But wait - the stable by the side
If you would . . .'
'Yes that will do fine
We cannot walk another stride.'
A child was born of a maid that night
And time was never again the same,
When in a stable long ago
An unexpected Saviour came.

And Christmas gifts and glad goodwill
Gain meaning from that joyous dawn,
When man was reconciled to man . . .
Nay! - when a child was born.

John M Davis

Christmas Fever

Once again, it's Christmas fever
Shopping, rushing, dashing there
Turkey, crackers, sweets and tinsel
Busy buying, purses bare.

It's a time when children sparkle
And excitement fills the air
People seem to be so friendly
No one seems to have a care.

But of course for some, it's different
Circumstance and age intrude
Enjoyment of the festive season
Just a trying interlude.

And for those who think it's humbug
An expensive waste of time
Who forget the real meaning
Doesn't have to cost a dime.

So let's remember other people
Not as fortunate as we
And try to celebrate this Christmas
The way it ought to be.

G Thomas

A Christmas City

All night snow fell
To a few inches depth
In large white flakes it fell
On the city brown;
Stealthily and loosely settling
Sifting and veiling roads, roofs and railings,
The latest traffic of the drowsy town
With all its murmurs seems drowned
In the silent foggy air all o'er;
From a high and frosty heaven
A wonderful brightness reveals
With the winter dawning,
A strange heavenly gleam appears
For it's the great day!
The eye marvels - marvels,
The school-going boys out in streets
In joy exuberant, awaiting
The great moments of Christmas!
The sun is out in pale display
Standing by St Paul's high dome,
The sun though sparkling
Seems fading in the atmosphere foggy,
He pours out in profusion upon streets
Thoroughfares and everywhere
Stirring the day to a life
Of unlimited joy and happiness!
To the church - they look so earnest
To welcome the blessed moments of the day.

Kalyan Ray

A Special Birthday

Cards are posted near and far
Christmas bands we can hear
Decorations on the wall
Gifts wrapped for one and all
Children will not sleep at night
Christmas morning is in sight
A baby born on Christmas night
Was sent to teach us wrong from right.

Christmas trees never stand
Far away in another land
No greeting card or Christmas band
Children with cold hands and toes
At Christmas time think of those
The 'Christmas Story' is unknown
There, no fire or telephone
Let warm hand reach out to cold
And the Christmas story told
So their future can unfold.

Sheila Walters

Seasonal Thoughts

Days are short and nights are long
Christmas is drawing near
I spare a thought for those who've gone
Those who I hold dear.

I think of good times that we shared
Of how they did their best
I think of how they are at peace
In their eternal rest.

Then I pick myself up, take a breath
And think of things soon to come
Like Christmas cheer, carollers song,
Gifts and family fun.

So then I sit back, raise a glass
And give thanks to God above
And send a Christmas message
To all my family, sent with love.

Douglas Andrew

Winter Sunshine

Everything's dead.
The trees, the flowers, the birds.
The animals are hibernating, waiting
Till the warmth of the sun welcomes them home.

On a single day.
In a little town named Bethlehem.
It is snowing,
A cold December night.

Suddenly a bright spark of light
Is born into the world.
To save us from dying like
The trees, the flowers and the birds.
It's the winter sunshine.

Sierra Gaffney (16)

The Bright Star

Christmas is the time of happiness,
Of laughter, fun and joy,
But let us not forget to celebrate, the birth,
Of a very special baby boy.

That baby, who was born in a stable,
The nearby inn was full that night,
As he was born, a bright star appeared,
A shimmering, gleaming ray of light.

There were three travellers, who were wise,
Travelling that night from afar,
They were awaiting news of that special child
When suddenly they saw the star.

A star so bright it lit up the sky,
Guiding the travellers on their way,
At their journey's end, they saw the baby,
Sleeping contentedly on the hay.

The travellers, spread their gifts around the crib,
Where the baby lay, so snug and warm,
Then they spread the news both far and wide,
That the Son of God that night was born.

So let the bells ring out, with a joyful peel,
In celebration of that wondrous sight,
Then say a prayer for all the world,
That peace may prevail, upon this holy night.

Then as the bells fall silent,
May God bless you, each and everyone,
Let there be peace within your hearts
And may the next year be a happy one.

Maud Eleanor Hobbs

Christmas

It's that time again for presents and fun
But we must not forget how it began
A little baby to show us the way
So in our thoughts He should stay
It's not just a time for food and drink
We can enjoy ourselves but stop sometimes and think
That seems to be fair
If it wasn't for *Him*
We would not be here.

J Taylor

The Joy Of Christmas

This time has come when days grow cold
Your merry hearts have turned to gold
For winter has appeared again
It's Christmas time we say Amen.

The joy of Christmas all around
There's snow and ice upon the ground
There's little children round the tree
Their eyes light up for all to see.

A time to share your joy and glee
With friends so old and folks in need
But don't forget this time of year
For Jesus was born a baby dear.

With that my friends I'd like to say
On this our one and special day
Let's raise a glass to all, let's say
Good luck, good health in every way.

R Claxton

Xmas

Xmas time is almost here
How I wish it was not as near
I have so many gifts to buy
Can't think what to get, no matter how I try.

I now know what to do, I'm pleased to say
Money for some, tokens for others so that they
Can buy what they want, something to read
Or a video to play, they can purchase what they need.

Mary Crickmore

Christmas 2006

On TV, Santa strolls in a snowy street,
White-whiskered and moustached,
With a smile, all and sundry to greet
Carrying a sack, so none a present shall lack,
To a child he gives two bottles of Coca-Cola!
Years later, the child returns his favour,
Coca-Cola, so Santa got his own back!
Then realise, on reflection, we've
Been 'had' by an 'ad' a conclusion passing sad
Never thus, when this poet was a lad
Then see how this does Christmas commercialise
Yet typical of our time, in other ways sublime.

Christmas cards flow in and for
Festive greetings, we have a thirst
We're not slow in replying,
Often coming first!
Holy themes not forgot, but
Seasonal themes fill the pot.
See robins in the snow, carollers
Fingers, feet and faces all aglow
Singing, bringing jingle bells in the snow,
Nothing is quite so quiet and clean
As snow falling on a holy night.
Chestnuts roast on the fire,
Raise a toast of laughter never tire,
Wishing till - bells would
Be temporarily still - bells.
Materialism the tale it tells.

Then, suddenly pause thinking
Some kids and kin never see Santa Claus.
When in the west, people enjoy the best
Whilst elsewhere, famine, war
And death never rest.

Whilst all remember dead friends,
Still able to celebrate Heaven's blessings,
Jesus present beside our hearth
Where comes the next meal, no guessing.

G Watkins

Santa's Mishap

Santa Claus was busy in his workshop last night
Wrapping lots of presents and making sure they looked all right.
Tomorrow would be a busy day, sorting out his sleigh
And getting all the reindeer fed before they started on their way.

Santa yawned a great enormous yawn and stumbled off to bed
He started drifting off to sleep before the pillow met his head
Bright and early in the morning his alarm clock started ringing
And little robin redbreast came to the window singing.

Santa reached out for his teeth but his teeth had disappeared
I wonder where they are? he thought as he rubbed his beard
Santa started searching, but time was getting on
He had still a lot of things to do and already half the day was gone.

Mrs Claus, she kept on searching from morning through to night
But everywhere she looked no false teeth were in sight
Then Santa had a horrid thought, he hoped he wasn't right
Had his teeth got muddled up with the gifts the other night?

So please be very careful and keep both eyes open wide
In case you open up a present and find Santa's teeth inside.

J L Preston

Christmas Cheer

Christmas comes just once a year
Full of fun and festive cheer
From smiling kids with lovely gifts
To families having Christmas rifts
The TV is full of Santa's face
A month before the fun takes place
Office parties come and go
Snogging folk you hardly know
With people not so used to drink
Spending all next day by the bathroom sink
TV is full of things we know
With repeats of many 'classic' shows
My wife says I just sit around
As she stops the season ship from going 'aground'
From cards to gifts to Christmas Day
Though she wouldn't have it any other way!
Before we know it the kids will be grown up and gone
So we'll enjoy our constant and growing family bond
And I hope our feelings for each other always last
Cemented with our memories of Christmases past.

Chris Leith

The Observer

So this is Christmas,
It's rolled round again.
Can't say I'm glad to see it,
But it makes a change you know.

The tinsel and the baubles
Twinkle cheaply on their trees,
Admired by spoilt children.
Shame their joy won't last forever.

I've observed the tiresome families,
Parading up and down the streets.
They hate each other really,
But are in it for the gifts.

I suppose that it's tradition,
To be around one's friends.
I've decided I'll comply
And get together with the boys.

We'll crack some jokes and have a laugh,
Eat mince pies and drink mulled wine
But they're odd mates I've got tonight,
The street, the snow and frosty skies.

Emma Grant

Untitled

The more important is spirit of Christian
Is expansive, expressive, exteriorisation of union fraternity
Beauty, sentiment to one example is voracity
We are brothers of blood for build love
True poem, simple theme, Christian
Gift to human body celeste
Light of dream and temperance
Love to all we!

Edemilson Reis (17)

Starlight

One Christmas Eve long, long ago
A wondrous star shone down
It flooded the snow-covered Earth with light
Till it rested o'er Bethlehem town
Joseph tried for a room at the inn
But there was no room to be found
The star moved on and they followed it
To a stable dark and forlorn
Where Mary the virgin gave birth to a son
And Jesus our saviour was born.

Wrapped in swaddling clothes he lay
In a manger filled with straw
Where Mary and Joseph watched over him
To keep him safe and warm
Church bells rang out and angels sang
To tell the good news to all men
Three kings from the east rode to Bethlehem
Bearing gifts so fine and rare
They fell to their knees as they offered the King
Gifts of gold, frankincense and myrrh.

Shepherds came down from the hills
With their gift of a newborn lamb
Oxen and ass came wandering in
As a chorus of angels sang
Now every year the story is told
To both the young and the old
Of the night when the holy child was born
To bring peace and goodwill to all men
All over the land songs of praise are sung
To welcome the infant King
So Come All Ye Faithful, rejoice and join in
A great and glorious Amen!

Pat Booker

Christmas Yorkshire Puddings

Delicious at Christmas
I could not find a turkey
Anywhere: I had hot
Yorkshire puddings
For Christmas: delicious!

Edmund Saint George Mooney

The Aftermath

Christmas is over
The guests have all gone
You look at the debris
And realise you are alone.
The holly is dropping
There's rubbish galore
You go to the kitchen
And look at the floor.
My *god,* was it worth it
This feasting and fooling
How come this is Christmas
By whose standard and ruling?
The scene was a stable
The cradle a stall
Why has it changed
To this 'grabber' takes all?
What is the message
For this day and age?
Just keep on buying
Whatever's the rage.
Make someone richer
By fleecing the poor
Make next year different
By locking your door.

Pat Adams

Erylene And Stuart's Christmas Tree

Your Christmas tree stands tall,
Its lights shine the brightest of all,
Beautifully decorated with love and care,
I can't help but stand and stare.

I have never seen such a tree before,
I could look at it for evermore,
Lost in this special tree, that says so much to me,
The delight in my eyes you must surely see.

I wish the tree could stay all year,
Seeing it makes me want to give a big cheer,
Your tree watches everything and becomes a part of you,
And when I'm there I share it too.

Julie Marie Laura Shearing

Merry Christmas To You

Christmas, not far away - approaches, dragging feet
Fears, holly and mistletoe, chicken, turkey, sides of meat.

Dislikes ribbons and bows, expensive useless gifts
Avoids greedy children, whose pendulum never shifts.

Abhors beer and spirits, refuses to gorge upon food
Wishes to enter our world in a simple holy mood.

Adores a quiet birth, amongst angels and wise kings
Loves this 'child' of God brought by messengers with wings.

Praise, honest adoration in such a lovely meek place
Spreads peace to us all living under His grace.

Think of Christmas as holy, abandon thoughts of money
Give to those who have nothing, poverty definitely not funny.

God will then bless you, guide you all though your life
Make your heart full of love, thus avoiding hate's knife.

Merry Christmas to you.

Maureen Westwood O'Hara

The First Christmas Day

As I looked out upon the morn,
On the day the great God's Son was born,
Even the sun seemed to kneel and pray
When it rose from the edge
Of the world today
All the birds seem to wait
Not even a twitter, not even a song
They all seemed to know
To whom this great day belonged
The wind seemed to still into a breeze
As though to be kind to the flowers and trees
The star in the east was twinkling with joy
As it remembered the birth
Of the great Father's boy
The life of our saviour
Had indeed now begun
And thank God for His Son
On the first Christmas Day.

V N King

Christmas Wish To Santa

Light as a feather from a dove
A snowflake fell on me with love
I stood there wondering, could be
A little sign, message for me.

I held the snowflake in my hand
And made a wish that it could grant
A spark of hope that it'll come true
And blew my wish back, Santa to you.

When the sun shone in harmony
On the chilly Christmas morning
I looked up above my head to see
The colour palette's drawing.

And what I saw, I couldn't describe
Nor could I believe my rainbow eyes
Magic or not, I couldn't decide
The nature of this wonderful surprise.

I stood there staring at the sky
Colours of the morning gleaming
Now I know all it takes is faith and love
Hope, and of course . . . believing.

Angela Mesropean

So, This Is Christmas

Months come and go and time passes by,
Soon it will be Christmas, is the cry.
Preparing two or three months ahead,
With the shops enthusiasm, we are led!

Slowly excitement creeps all around,
Dates for panto's and Xmas meals are found,
Selecting cards keeps one busy,
Writing and 'posting early' sends one dizzy.

Presents for family and each special friend,
The rush has started, when will it end?
Wrapping and writing busily to everyone,
And loads of food to order before it's all done.

To warmer climates some folks fly,
But everything is different, one cannot deny.
Many are unable this excitement to share,
Elderly alone with memories and a silent prayer,
Face another TV Christmas, sat in their favourite chair.

Peace on Earth - goodwill to all men,
When will this message happen, when, when, when?

Stella Bush-Payne

Christmas

Christmas is a time for caring,
Giving, receiving and for sharing.
The house trimmed up, the tree is lit,
The cards are ready and specially writ.

The wrapping on gifts is ready to tear
Joy and happiness we all do share.
Parties to go to, outfits to find
Enjoyment of being so wined and dined.

We all share a moment for the less fortunate and poor
Thinking of those who are still out at war.
Wanting to help, to charity we do give
Hoping we're helping someone else live.

Christmas Eve and time for bed
Each child grabs their duvet and covers their head.
Excited they wait for the moment to come
To find out if Santa has drunk all his rum.

The morning is here and yes he has been
Never seen the children fast up and looking so keen.
We open the presents with all of our might
Everyone's faces are filled with delight.

Time for dinner, Dad carves up the roast
While Mum pours the wine, ready for toast.
Pulling of crackers and party hats on
Time when the family does become one.

Night arrives, oh what a hectic day
Though none of us would have it any other way.
We all do enjoy this festive season
And we thank the Lord Jesus, as he is the reason.

Nina Gwatkin

An Enchanted Winter Night

Crisp winter air, a crunchy covering of snow,
Children play, muffled in scarves and gloves, as snowmen grow.
A landscape altered, as winter settles his icy blast,
Cosy by the fire, minds wander back to Christmas past.

Twinkling fairy lights decorate the tree,
In the deep dark winter, faces illuminated by thoughts of He,
Who, down the chimney soon will climb,
While silently winter nights whisper away with each clock chime.

Mince pies and cream, mulled wine and eggnog,
Is that the tinkle of sleigh bells in the fog?
Excitement and glee on Christmas Eve
A night of enchantment when all in the magic believe!

Caroline Shanks

The Forgotten Christmas

Christmas is fast approaching
Let hearts be blessed with cheer
Yet, embrace each other with kindness
As we witness another passing year.

Santa's sleigh has replaced the manger
Flying reindeer replaced the ass
That Mary journeyed so long upon
To fulfil what was to pass.

Even stamps show not the manger now
But Santa sat upon a roof
Are the post office denying the childbirth
Or for profit ignoring the truth?

'Mistletoe and Wine' is the song to sing
As Mary's boy child takes a back seat
Even 'Come All Ye Faithful'
Appears a carol to cower in defeat.

The angel atop a glistening tree
Is replaced by a fairy or toy
Such drinking and gluttony amid Christmas time
Forsakes the true Christian joy.

Without the birth of Jesus
There would be no Christmas time
To forsake the birth of our salvation
Under Heaven - is the ultimate crime.

So please bring back our Christmas
Liken to days of old
When the birth was our celebrations
Not Santa or reindeer gold.

At Christmas we should honour Him
And sing our praise out loud
Not drink and fill our belly
But in gratitude stand up proud.

Steve Kettlewell

World Of White

As the sun outside finally went to sleep and fell
Another element slowly came, with its own story to tell

All through the night they blissfully slept unaware
That white magic began to fall around and everywhere

A day so cold yet so warm, would tomorrow yield such treasure
The morning delight would bring a beautiful gift from Mother Nature

As young children sleep in their beds they peacefully dream
Yet all is calm and still in the outside world it would seem

Morning has arrived, the new day has dawned and the blanket
of white is deep
Presents are enjoyed and families rejoice, then outside into snow
the children leap

Deeper and further they tread, through snow with delight
All of winter's fruit, they have savoured, for long a day and night.

Karim Hetherington

Twenty-Fifth

What to you does Christmas mean?
Is it a child to a virgin born
Or a gift from a gent in red?

What to you does Christmas mean?
Is it a feast of foods so fair
Or a rest from work's hard toil?

What to you does Christmas mean?
Is it a gleeful childish squeal
Or a joyous sacred mass?

What to you does Christmas mean?
Is it a line of glittering cards
Or a roll of ribbon gold?

What to you does Christmas mean?
Is it a star that burned so bright
Or a gathering of loved ones dear?

What to you does Christmas mean?
Is it a cracker snapping gaily
Or logs popping on the fire?

What to you does Christmas mean?
Is it a frantic shopping spree
Or a berry red on a holly bract?

Some things have many answers
Some things have none at all.
Some answers lie within your heart
Some lie beyond your grasp.
Some guidance I now have for you
Some important note to heed.
Let someone know you care this year
Let someone know you're there.

Ceri DD Griffiths

Christmas Chimes

Was it not the angels' song
Upon recorded carols played
That multicoloured heavenly
The lights on Mow Cop's breezy hill?
Are we not the shepherds still?
We nurse rejected, outcast lamb
That is the good news of a birth
Drowned out by ring of checkout tills
Drunk out of consciousness of those
Who seek refuge in headache pills
Since there is no great escape
From the frantic rush that kills

From the slope enkindled plain
In awe, the yellow polka dots
Are inspired by the flickering dance
Playing on Santa's stars and sleighs
Round balls, up ladders, many things
In the hush, do you not hear
The fluttering of angels' wings?
Does not your heart give you the beat
Of tune that divine herald sings?
If this a task too long deferred
Your staff will help you down from peak
To spread with joy what you have heard.

David Speed

The Joy Of Christmas

Long ago in a stable,
The Son of God was born,
To save mankind for Heaven,
When they were all forlorn.

No flowers bloomed around him,
Just humble beasts were there,
Their breath warmed all around him,
That babe beyond compare.

The years may pass as minutes,
The sun and moon grow dim,
But none shall show us loving,
As deep and true as him.

So gather round the manger,
And quietly say a prayer,
His love secure around you,
There's nothing left to fear.

Mary Hughes

Christmas Eve

As winter is upon us
The sky becomes a white sheet
A chill seeps through the air
And snowflakes descend on the land.

There is a snuffle and a rustle
A hedgehog shuffles across the grass
He shivers and quivers in the mist
And hunts for food in the soil.

Through every window, a tree stands tall
Its lights twinkle and glow in the dark
Presents gather together under the tree
And await tomorrow's excitement.

Each child sleeps, there is no sound
Mums and dads prepare the turkey
But in the silence, anticipation rises
And cards perch proudly on the mantel.

A snowman stands on the snow in the frosty garden
His buttons slide down his front
He dreams of a friend being built tomorrow
And his arms sway in a light wind.

As all becomes quiet, no noise to be heard
Sleigh bells sound in the distance
Reindeer sweep through the sky and land on each roof
And Santa slides down every chimney to find milk and mince pies.

He creeps through each house, to find the tree
And leaves gifts for all who are good
As he fills each stocking he chuckles softly
And collects carrots for Rudolph and co.

Muffled cries can be heard from somewhere above
As Santa continues his journey
He calls encouragement to his reindeer, so that they fly
And admires the snow scene below.

As dawn arrives, birds begin to sing
People begin to stir
Broad smiles cover each and every face
And calls of 'Merry Christmas' echo all around.

Harriet Elizabeth Hobbs (14)

The Yule Machine

The snowman
Is about
To make his lips quiver
And sing me a carol
I wrote him

The tree of last year
Is about
To open the gift
I gave him

The indifferent girl in the greeting card
Is about
To return the glance
I gave her

And I'm about
To close my eyes
And celebrate.

Pushpraj Singh

Heaven's Treasure

Now I see what I longed to see
Heaven's treasure falling down on me
Slowly from the thick smoke they descend
And now I know that Christmas has come
But this feeling makes me cry.

I can perceive the fragrance of Christmas
A smell that is different from home
I stare at Heaven and plead
Hoping it wouldn't last forever
And this thought makes me cry.

Is Heaven's treasure here to stay?
Is it trying to make me happy?
Now I hear sweet voices from Heaven singing
'Jungle bells, jingle bells,'
And truly this song makes me cry.

This time last year we were together
Singing these songs that made me glad
Now I am standing on Heaven's treasure
And I wish it will last forever
But this wish makes me cry.

Ndidi Ubogu

Memories

The room was festive with tinsel and tree,
Windows patterned with artificial snow.
The old woman, dozing quietly in her chair
Dreamed of Christmases she'd known long ago.

Red-nosed, numb-fingered, carol singers arrive,
Accepting mince pies before singing once more.
The Midnight Mass in the peaceful old church,
We exchange season's greetings with friends at the door.

Mulled wine, log fires, real candles on the tree,
Children opening stockings; excited laughter loud.
Holly and mistletoe and clandestine kisses,
Relatives come; we're now quite a crowd.

The family all sitting around the large table
Laden with turkey, stuffing and sprouts.
Mum brings in the pudding, engulfed in blue flame.
'We must make a wish,' young Sally shouts.

Uncle Jim, dressed as Santa, hands out the presents.
There's one, large or small, for everyone there.
Then we sit quietly to hear the Queen's speech,
Though Grandad has fallen asleep in the chair.

A yell of excitement, it's snowing at last.
It's settling and should be quite deep by the dawn,
Promising snow fights and scary toboggan slides
And an army of snowmen guarding the lawn.

'Come on now, Ada, I've brought you your cocoa,'
The care nurse said gently. 'I think it's a shame
That you have to spend Christmas here in the home.'
Ada just smiled, and - lost in the past - merely smiled again.

Gwen Hoskins

At Year's End

In the festive season to be jolly
When time is sparing and the deadly threat
Of chemical warfare and terror looms
It is not Christmas, but the mellow songs
Of birds chorusing like angels, that bring
True joy and hallelujah harmony

It is the fresh ocean breezes with warm
Winds in my hair and the salty smell of
Wild seas that makes me thirsty, yearn for your
Sun-kissed energy, your natural charm

It is the feel of the blue rolling waves
And the sensing of the tides, the roaring
Eddying, spume and spray against craggy
Starfished rocks on this special Christmas Day

Alone, with friendly dolphins I will swim
Splish, splash, till sunset's final red dot sinks
Where reflected lights on waters shine as
Shimmering diamonds in this summer's night

Reluctantly, I'll be thinking of you
Your country's coldness, brittle ice and snow
Rugged up, afar in glistening white landscapes
Of sparkling crystalled pines and skipping deer

Here and forever, the blue wrens and the
Scarlet robins still sing. They sing sweetly
Clearly, of peace and love for you, for me
We pray that sanity will rule the way.

Barbara A Taylor

Christmas, Or Is It?

The three wise men they travelled
Following a bright new star
No thought for them of an iPod
Game Boy or Scalextrix car.

They came to seek a newborn King
Lying in a manger there
No traffic queues for M&S
Or finding the train fare.

They travelled with their camels
Across a desert wide
Not for them Chelsea tractors
Gleaming and polished with pride.

They brought along gifts of myrrh
Gold and frankincense
Not DVDs or CDs
Nor posh designer scents.

They travelled by day and night
To a town called Bethlehem
Not London, Cardiff, Newcastle
Or trendy Cheltenham.

They walked into a cattle shed
To a manger lined with hay
No modern, high-tech, maternity suite
Or fathers on paternity pay.

They saw baby Jesus lying there
Wrapped in swaddling bands
No labels from Marie Chantal
Dressed by Nannie's hands.

To them this was true Christmas
A time of joy and love
No Christmas tree and turkey
But a gift from God above.

Bryan Evans

Christmas Time

Christmas time looms once again
So often filled with stress and strain
To give a gift with our love
As did our heavenly Father above.

The reason for this time of cheer
So often lost as burdens bear
Too much pressure this material goal
Remember to feed your spiritual soul.

C S Cyster

The News

Christmas bells across the meadow
Spread the news of joy on Earth
Pealing o'er the frosty landscape
Telling of the Saviour's birth.

Cattle kneeling in the byre
Up above, a radiant star
Perfect love has come among us
Spread the word both near and far.

Trudging through the winter weather
On the way to midnight mass
Old and young with smiling faces
Shout a greeting as they pass.

For Christ was born at Christmas
The herald angels sing
To bring us peace and joy on Earth
Our Saviour and our King.

Janet Cavill

The Wind

The wind it howls all through the night
My mind it wanders out of sight
To a long-gone time when we were fine
And nothing could our love untwine.

Oh Christmas future, present and past
I think I knew our love couldn't last
And that I would lament lashed to the mast
About a long-lost love in Christmas past.

Fairy lights and shining stars
Busy, noisy public bars
Santa Claus and flashing trees
My memories have all of these and you.

Who went away one summer's day
No more you and I to play
Now I'm lost in the winter sun
Christmas Day has just begun.

David Bennett

Untitled

The snow is white upon the ground
And you can hear a happy sound
Sleigh bells ringing, carol singing
Joy and goodwill all around.

Getting ready for the day
Celebrating, bright and gay
Children waiting, anticipating
Santa Claus has heard them say
A doll, a boat, a motor car
Games and toys brought from afar
And their faces on that morning
Will outshine the brightest star.

Carmel Allison

Gathering Of The Clan

At some quiet moment, around this time of year
I will ponder awhile, and shed a tear
For days which compare, to the finest wine
And above which, the stars did shine.

I'll remember the piano, playing many tunes
I'll remember the many different coloured balloons
I'll remember the drums with their heavy beat
And Christmas greetings, shouted in the street.

I'll remember the enjoyment ringing in the air
The snacks that were made, such wonderful fare
The smiling faces when we opened the door
A seasonal time, the clan gathered once more

The pleasure of voices, always to be heard
The sandwiches made from a well-cooked bird
The beat of pop groups, as records were played
Though time seems to vanish, memories never fade.

Piles of presents, which never seemed to end
Given by someone special, a traditional friend
Pairs of hands, tearing at Christmas wrapping
Constant amusement from young voices yapping.

Wherever you glanced there was excitement galore
Many pairs of feet waiting to jive on the floor
Such pleasure reverberated throughout that dwelling
Infectious amusement from jokes people were telling.

The Christmas tree brought from its hiding place
The foldaway kind, not one we had to replace
From each branch, decorations would hang
Pulling Christmas crackers, awaiting the bang.

Some do not have this pleasure, which we often recall and treasure
Locked away, are pictures I scan when we had a gathering
                                        of the clan.

B W Ballard

Our Christmas Gift

Hustling, bustling round the shops
People everywhere
Trees bright with tinsel
Lights how they glare
Counting down to Christmas
Drinking, parties, noise
Buying, buying, spending
On huge extravagant toys
Hush and give a thought
For our true Christmas gift
Our Lord and Saviour born this night
Our hearts that shall uplift
How joyous for this precious time
In the silence of the night
In a meagre stable lay a babe
He is our true light
Jesus born in Bethlehem
To save us all from sin
Come let us celebrate
And give our love to him.

Catherine Armstrong

Central Ceremonies

Do we automatically perform on special occasions?
Exchange greetings, enjoy December 25th with full realisation
Of why we celebrate Christmas in winter season
Or entertain serious thought toward basic reasons?

Winter months retain this seasonal break
To praise the Lord of existence, honouring the state
Of power and majesty, to whom we owe allegiance.
Every breath depends entirely on His merciful lenience.

During these days of quiet or jolly celebrations
Remember the less fortunate, homeless, hungry, destitute, forsaken.
Scratching heads, furrowed brows
Meaning problems ahead, puzzles now.
In subsequent years it'll be repeated
Seasonal bustle as Christmas preparations are completed.

Season of good cheer, it's alleged to bring
Nerves and emotions often taut like fiddle strings.
Frenzied shopping, what will I buy?
Multiple choice, close my eyes and try
To visualise the perfect gift
For presenting to new family, born on the twenty-fifth
A future heir to the local magician
Complexion fair, in perfect condition.

Long ago a baby appeared
Born in a manger by few revered.
No fuss before birth for this special babe.
Without preparation, he was gently laid by
Mary and Joseph, the privileged guardians
Of a future Saviour, sent by his Father
Redeemer, Counsellor, Mighty One
Give thanks and praise God for gifting His precious Son.

Annie Harcus

That Wonderful Feeling

There's a wonderful feeling steals into your heart
When the season called Christmas is near
It makes your heart glow
But we really don't know where it comes from
It comes every year.
It must be the love that came from above
To that stable in Bethlehem town
And it comes once again to steal into your heart
As silently now it comes down.
It makes strangers seem friends
And that love never ends
As once more it steals into your heart
At this time of the year when it brings Christmas cheer
And of us it will always be part.

Margaret B Baguley

Jesus Came

Jesus came from Heaven above
To share with us God's wondrous love
He is the life, the truth, the way
The God of this and every day.

Straw in a manger was His bed
Nowhere soft to lay His head
Sheep and cattle looking on
At the birth of God's own Son.

Shepherds from the hills around
And eastern kings on holy ground
Knelt, in wonder and in awe
At all the things they heard and saw.

This baby grew into a man
Fulfilling God's eternal plan
Dying for lost humanity
Including such as you and me.

So let's come and celebrate Christ's birth
The life He lived down here on Earth
He died for sin, He took our part
But lives again in yielded hearts.

David Clark

It's Christmas

Australian snow blew into Windsor
the first to find the town this year
It must be rare
and generous to share some snow with us in Britain
especially in their summer
although on a greeting card.

In the picture was a kangaroo
with cold stuff on his feet
covering a lot of footage
and not allowed to look perplexed at all in print
standing like refrigerated animal.

Summer never is the same for kangaroos
since people came from Britain
even if they stand upright and hop to music
but transportation snow
should not have come at all.

How can you tell a kangaroo
all else is second place to Christmas.

Reg Baggs

Christmas

Christmas
The birth of Christ
Still a celebration
Saint Nick now known as Santa Claus
The children's eyes are bright this Christmas Eve
Stockings, holly and mistletoe
Gifts and family fun
Merry, merry . . .
Christmas.

Sarah Louise Hudson

At Christmas Time

I'd like to splash the water
In Trafalgar Square
On the hour
With you my dear
At Christmas time.

I'd like to skate on ice
In Central Park
With you my dear
At Christmas time.

I'd like to light the lights
On Sydney Bridge
Then disappear
With you my dear
At Christmas time.

But most of all
I'd like to kiss you, hug you, hold you near
At Christmas time my dear!

Christian Schou

Christmas, Christmas

Here again
Bright lights and
Food everywhere

Seeing all your
Family and friends
Having a good time

Opening presents
Getting
What you like

Cannot wait
Till next year
When Christmas happens
Again.

Bav

Christmas

(This poem can be sung to the tune of 'Jesus loves me, this I know, for the Bible tells me so')

Christmas is a time of cheer
Boys and girls are glad it's here
Everyone should kneel and pray
And thank God for Christmas Day.

Glory and honour
Glory and honour
Glory and honour
To Him who died for sin.

Christmas Day comes once a year
Reminding us God's Son came here
Down from Heaven to Earth He came
Praise and honour to His name.

Everyone should really know
Why God sent His Son below
Jesus came to die for sin
And save all who trust in Him.

Jesus is the name God gave
To His Son who came to save
At His feet we all must fall
And confess Him Lord of all.

Samuel McAlister

A Star Of Hope

A star of hope shines in our sky
Though we may wonder why
There is such turmoil, so much strife
Within this world with troubles rife.
This star shone over Bethlehem
Heralding one who wears a diadem -
The Christ-child in the manger
Who to many is but a stranger,
Yet he comes to every heart
Inviting all to have a part
Of his glorious kingdom's reign
Which through the cross all may gain
Where he shall rule in splendour
With love's sceptre; just, fair and tender,
The Prince of Peace, who's glory
Is the great unchanging story.

Stanley Birch

Xmas 2006

Well, it's here at last - the 24th December
I've been ready for this since the 12th of November
Plum puddings are bought - Mathew Walker you know
And all I need now are some robins and snow.
The mince pies are made and the trifle looks good
This Xmas will be, as all Christmas should.
No queues for me, I've organised well
Every present is wrapped and don't they look swell.
The tree is all trimmed - has been since November
Now is there anything else I have to remember?
Yes, there my eyes on the stable did fall
With Mary and baby - the heart of it all.
What matters the robins - what matters the snow?
For on Christmas morning, to church I will go
And there I will kneel and there I will find
The *true* meaning of Christmas and *peace to mankind.*

Madge Bourne

The Season's Greeting

Once a season to be jolly
Now we may not hang up holly.
Does this mean we are unable
To stand on desktop or table?
Legs of the latter too unsteady
But - decorations are ready.
Well, here's something to make you gladder
The lads have found this stepladder.

Management fears an accident.
They still don't know where profits went
Though to the boss, a bonus due
Oh he is afraid someone will sue?
For all this tinsel his staff yearn
Are Health and Safety his concern?

So - what does our adviser say?
No - don't all shrug and stalk away
Now we're forbidden mistletoe!
It distracts the workshy who go
To kiss each other under it.
Go hang it where the boss must sit!

Of course, he's careful to explain
He wants no woman to complain
About harassment. Not like last year
When male colleagues drank too much beer.
They say they still can't understand
How their party got out of hand.

Boss and board at their last meeting
Sent us all their season's greeting
Though they've made it must less jolly
Without mistletoe and holly.

Chris Creedon

When Daddy Swallowed The Sixpence

When Daddy swallowed the sixpence there was such a hullabaloo
It brightened the gloom of the long afternoon
And gave us all something to do.

We were spending the day with Mum's parents
They were glum and respectable folk
Children, they inferred, should be seen and not heard
So we sat there and none of us spoke.

The long silent lunch was completed
On slices of pudding we fed
Gran made sure each one had a sixpence with some
Waxed paper tied round it with thread.

Grandmother looked round the table
For the ending of dinner to call
On each plate was spread waxed paper and thread
But on Dad's plate was nothing at all.

'What have you done with your sixpence?'
Mum's question was shrill with concern.
'What sixpence?' he said.
'Oh my God, he'll be dead. Quick, quick, we must make it return.'

Well Grandpa was patting his back
To make the sixpence he swallowed come out.
Gran ran to the sink to get him a drink
While we kids were just leaping about.

The rest of the day was quite jolly
And Dad, he enjoyed all the fuss.
In all the excitement the grandparents brightened
And stopped disapproving of us.

Well, going home Dad gave a chuckle
And to our amazement took out
A sixpenny packet from inside his jacket,
'Was this what the fuss was about?'

Philippa Bower

Hope

The chandelier
Hangs bright and clear
In the middle of the hall.

The guests arrive
Upon the drive
Ready for the ball.

A welcome light
Spills into the night
Greeting one and all.

The party goes on
Till everyone's gone
And silence descends like a wall.

The tramp at the gates
Watches and waits
In the hope that good fortune will fall.

Ann Dawes-Clifton

Christmas Spirit

This is the tale of a little tree
No resemblance to the Christmas variety
Been growing in Dave's garden - well only just
For many a month - without any fuss.

When up spoke Dave's wife - a sprightly lass
Who thought of saving a bit of brass
That tree - with a star and a 'lick of paint'
Could be made to look - what it really 'aint.

Now Dave a brave lad most of the time
Couldn't face his wife, couldn't step out of line
Crept into the garden, one winter night
Fixed a star on the tree - before first light.

He sprayed it all over with glitter and gold
On that dark winter night in the freezing cold
Then fled black indoors to resume the good life
To his beer and his baccy and now loving wife.

H Hayward

Who'd Had Thought It?

Turkey's cooking nicely
Whiffs of spices and mulled wine
Paper hats and crackers
Yes, everything seemed fine.

Just a case of waiting
To greet the family
Time to wrap the presents
To place around the tree.

Robert was the first to phone,
'Mum, the A-road's closed
We can't see how to make it
Because of drifting snows.'

Soon after came a message
Our Jim and Sal had flu
I eyed the cat who eyed me back,
'Well, dinner then for two.'

'Twas then I had a brainwave
Washed tearstains from my face
I'd wrap the food in plastic packs
Rescue it from waste.

Placed the bags into my car
Went on my way alone
The Sally Army's open house
For folks without a home.

They welcomed me with open arms
Invited me to stay
Embraced me with a kindness
Oh happy Christmas Day!

Kathleen Faulkner

Christmas

I went into a very big store
I saw Christmas presents galore
What can I get for Aunty Rose?
Perhaps an anchor for her turned up nose.

And for my uncle Ted?
A moustache wash, after he's fed
For my little cousin Ruth
A new, shiny, false tooth.

A special present for my mum
A hammer to flatten her tum
For my dad to stop his snore
He really is quite a bore.

For my big brother Bryn
Something to make him grin
Medicine for my grandad
To stop him feeling so bad.

For my gran, I have not forgot
A fan so she wouldn't be so hot
For Christmas Day I cannot wait
I'm only a little girl of eight.

Mavis Shaw

Warm Beginnings

Cold is the winter
Deep is the snow
Frozen water
That cannot flow.

Shadow of an angel
All in white
The joy of Christmas
In the night.

Unto us
A child is born
Lying in a manger
Soft and warm.

Pretty paper
Of red and blue
Seasons greetings
For me and you.

In a Sunday service
The choir is singing
Christ the Saviour
With bells ringing.

David Eastment

A Christmas Wish

A Christmas wish, good fortune and cheer
If only it lasted throughout the year
Health and happiness is worth more than gold
Especially when you're growing old.

If that bright star once more would shine
We could be sure the world was fine
Kings and shepherds, one and all
Rejoice and sing around the stall.

Snow is falling, silent the night
As we all pray for peace and right
Throughout the world, to everyone
Let's pray for peace when day is done.

To everyone, let's wish them joy
Each child to have a Christmas toy
Think of others, life can be cruel
As we celebrate this time of Yule.

Think well before you ask for more
What you have got, you can be sure
Tis more than most, less than a few
Good wishes at Christmas, God bless you.

Keith Willmott

The Other Side Of Christmas

Happy families with well-filled bellies
Huddled around their widescreen tellies
Celebrating they know not what
Well into the night.

Outside the dark roads glitter
As a hard night's frost takes hold
Lone figure in shop doorway at war against the cold
Looking out at the world through haunted eyes
At how it used to be
Wife and kids and jingle bells
Sparkling Christmas tree.

Early morning light on a cold wintry day
Another Christmas past
In the doorway of a charity shop
A loser breathes his last.

John Bilsland

Christmas Feeling

Spread of white
Spark of light
Chill in the air
Christmas time fayre.

Quiet and peace
Hat and a fleece
Fire all aglow
Sprinkling of snow.

Family arrives
Brightness of eyes
Tree full of lights
Favourite of nights.

Night without sleep
Tiptoe and peep
Handful of wishes
Thankyous and kisses.

Mary Daines

Christmas Eve

Shop work tiresome
The customers fled
A merry Christmas under muttered breath
Blinds down, till cashed
Another day's takings to be banked
Tho' tonight let be forgotten
On my part jobs can wait
Tonight the night of Christmas
Tonight my night of rest.

Other adults smile
And moan their family's traits
'Christmas not the same,' they say
Christmas just for kids
Adult's eyes, a tired frame
But the child still here inside
I nod my head, imitate, agree
But look a look of pity.

Little girl never grew up
And pray I never shall
Lock the doors but dream ahead
Of surprises not yet had
I slave away to make ends meet
My body cold and tired
But Christmas Eve, this soul's alive
Christmas is all to me.

Sarah Hutchinson

The Promised One

Bright red berries -
Christmas trees
Tinsel, frost and Christmas melodies
Father Christmas and his reindeer
Mince pies, sherry and children's stockings
Gaily wrapped parcels under the tree
Visits from other members of the family
All speak of childhood memories for me
But what of that time so long ago
For which we celebrate like this?
Two weary travellers on a long road
And at the end
No place to rest
But a cave kept
To shelter the animals.
Here on a dark night a baby was born
Heralding new life for all
Shepherds watching in the fields
Startled by a heavenly host
Telling them exciting news
That tonight in Bethlehem
Was born the One who was to come
To Israel
Emmanuel
Born for the world
To take away sin
The baby born at Bethlehem!

Christina Miller

Winter

Winter is gentle
caressing the trees to sleep.
Wind, an overture
to a quiet symphony
of white. Winter is gentle.

Icicles a curtain for fall.
Catacombs of ruts
in the frozen pavement.
Cars slide by. And the
window is an abstract painting.

Christmas comes gentle
like a kiss on your cheek.
Trees bow their bald heads
to the music winter brings.
Silent shadows on the snow.

Joanne Benford

The Virgin And The Shepherds

Mary welcomed that first Christmas morn
When Jesus was a baby born
Meagrely
Although some shepherds, busting down
Looked for a Saviour in the town
Eagerly.
The Virgin looked at them, amazed,
As they her tiny infant praised,
Dreamy-voiced;
And when they told her how sweet singing
Angels through the night came winging,
She rejoiced
That God had thus confirmed His word
That she first from the angel heard
Long ago!
Her child would in human hearts
Sow seeds of faith which from the start
She'd see grow
And the whole world, from shore to shore,
Would fear the breath of death no more;
And the grave crime
In which her Son would be crucified
Would make the Father justified
And glorified
All through time!

Dan Pugh

An Old-Fashioned Christmas

A welcoming warmth greeted everyone
Promising happiness and fun.
A Christmas tree stood in the hall
Decorated and very tall.
A traditional gift from the mistletoe
Awaited those who stood below.
Old arrivals with travelling rugs
Greeted gladly with love and hugs,
New arrivals wrapped up well
Were each presented with a bell.
Food in the cellar with the best wine
Stood on cold slabs and looked fine.
The turkey and the pudding too
Stood proudly there for us to view.
There were pies, soups and ham,
Trifles, marmalade and jam,
Nuts to crack, and crackers to pull
Food to eat until we were full.
Stockings were hung on each bed
Or a pillowcase instead.
We always celebrated Christ's birth
By worshipping with joy and mirth.

Margaret Nixon

Awesome Silence

(This poem was written in the moments precisely following the onset of the Christmas tsunami 2004 which washed away so many native and visiting people from the shores of South Asia and Ceylon. David Light, the author, is convinced that the quiver and premonition came exactly together with the tsunami, and the movements of the tectonic plates)

An awesome silence covers lately fallen snow.
Midnight now, the day that Christ was born so lowly,
For us the stillness blanketed with orange glow,
Two thousand years reflected down have gone so slowly.
Dense and murky fog does mark this birthday holy.
Black blood hangs down on pointed holly,
Marking years of human folly.

So still the night; this holy night.
A snow-topped lawn that bears no breath of sound,
Nor slightest movement from the icy ground.
The snow has lightly traced each twig of lace;
Gives frozen burden to each arching conifer within
This silent enclosed garden, that recedes to fog's obscurity.
The past unrecognised. An unknown future with no face.

Two thousand years since Christmas Day.
God makes an offer every time we pass this way.
But man ignores, preferring Mammon's lively clutch,
Turning stable into shopping mall and wise men's gifts to
Tinsel or electron's babble, feasting, singing, drinking rabble.
Extravagance and waste we see. God's patience is severely stretched.
What, indeed, will He do next?

Standing here on solid step,
Nothing, absolutely nothing, sways this night-time peace.
A moment for reflection. Gaze upon the world we've made.
If every spot on Earth were coated in preserving icy fog,
Perhaps we could begin again and set another course.
Take up a new philosophy, where violence and anger
Have no part. Give place to help and generosity,
With love to all humanity.

My feet upon this Earth grow cold,
Now midnight's past, I feel a trembling quiver
And through my bones there spreads a premonition's shiver.
This man-made world has surely had its day.
What must it take to wash it all away?
A new belief to banish old,
Where help for suffering neighbour is the need.
Mankind at last can prove his singularity of breed.

David Light

At This Time Of Year

At this time of year
It matters not what people say.
If you will choose the right way, the good way,
You will find peace for your souls
And your heart will never grow cold.
Christmas can be the season
And a reason for joy and goodwill.
Filling our hearts with desires to give,
Hoping to show family and friends
The right way to live, and to follow the true light,
Jesus Christ.
Materialism fades away,
Just like the end of a day.
Whereas Godly relationships are like pure gold,
Beauty to behold.
Christmas trees are soon stripped bare
Of their momentary glory,
Because they do not tell the real story
That God in His mercy and love
Sent His dear Son from above
To bring salvation's story.
Beginning in Bethlehem's stable bare,
With a vulnerable babe,
Through to the Cross
And God's heartbreaking loss,
For you and for me.
But then the glory of his Resurrection,
Jesus Christ our true Sacrifice.

Rita Cassidy

The Bells

Red robin sings
Ruffles its wings.

Church bells rhyme,
Ringing in time.

Crier cries out
These charms we don't doubt.

And so once again
Our spirits warmly dance
And children at play
This season enhance.

But remember the same;
The orphan's name,
The poor man's keep
The tortured's sleep.

For Christmas is here!
Bringing news of good cheer
Our promises keep -
Your love sincere!

Stephen Shutak

Christmas Dreams

Christmas is a time many dreams can come true
If you look to the stars, the sun or the moon
You may follow a road if you travel this light
To where a land in the sky is merry and bright.

Your hopes and your wishes are dealt with here
By a team of happy folk
Who in purest delight
Hustle and bustle to make Christmas just right.

The folk carry your wishes around in their hands
And when they find you asleep in your land
They bring you the magic of dreams come true
Sprinkling your wishes around the room.

Do not think though
That every wish shall be yours
But as long as you dream
You will not be ignored.

Beverley Forster

Santa's Visit

Ready for bed anticipation grows
Will Santa visit? No one knows
Have I been good? Have I been bad?
If Santa doesn't visit, I will be sad.

I lie in bed, eyes tightly shut
He won't visit Mum said if I've been bad
I listen and strain to hear any noise
But long to see Rudolph's red nose.

I must not stir and I must not peek
To do so now would be just weak
The milk is poured, the mince pies on plate
Oh let me sleep, it's getting late.

The morning comes, I jump out of bed
The only thought that fills my head
Will Santa have been or has he forgot?
It's very cold but let's hope not!

I look out the window, snow covers the ground
No footprints to indicate Santa's been around
I wake the others and rush downstairs
Their laughter and joy fills the air.

Santa has been! The feeling is great
Thank you Santa for being a mate
See you next year. Please get some rest
Happy New Year and all the best.

Christine Wallis

God's Son

Christmas is for everyone,
Christmas is about God's Son.
The sad and lonely hide away,
The children just want to play.
God sent Jesus to save the world,
Jesus is our King and Lord.
Sad or lonely try to pray,
On this blessed Christmas Day.
God knows that you are there,
He will keep you in His care.

Joan Williams

It's Christmas!

Snow is falling, children play,
Santa Claus is on his way.
Snowball fighting in the park.
Snowmen dancing after dark.
It's Christmas!

Carol singers, voices sweet,
Hassled shoppers with sore feet.
Ho! Ho! Ho! cries old Nick
Candy canes are sweet to lick.
It's Christmas!

Holly berries, mistletoe
Fingers numb, faces glow.
Excited children, eyes shut tight
Reindeer flying through the night
It's Christmas!

Daylight peeps through curtains drawn.
Here, at last, comes Christmas morn!
Wrapping paper everywhere
From presents opened without care.
It's Christmas!

Bethany Hay (11)

Christmas Shopping

It's December again, I think with a frown
Of the annual pilgrimage to town
Where it's not the bells but the tills that are ringing
As the shops cash in with the shoppers bring
- Their money.

Is it socks again for Uncle Fred?
Does Aunt's pot plant have to be red?
And no doubt the kids want expensive toys?
Granny pleads for much less noise - that's the joys
- Of Christmas.

And then there's the food - is it duck or turkey?
Don't chicken out - you might be lucky
Maybe the beef joints you'll have to chance
Unless they've been sent off to France!
- That's unlikely!

Maybe you'll sit down at the computer
They say this is the shop of the future
Why drag round the stores when the easier bet
Is to get down on your Internet,
- Get online!

You've spent many hours on the cards and greetings
Probably dreading the relatives meetings!
And pantry full of good food is bursting
And bottles galore to quench all the thirsting,
- Where's the Rennies?

Now having of these jobs completed
You're fatigued and funds are depleted
Have you missed anything or left undone?
Amidst all the outward frolics and fun
- Of Christmas?

I *wonder* if He - lowly born in a manger
Is personally still to you just a stranger?
Remember He loves you - gave all for sin died
So return His love - be found at the side
- Of Jesus, this Christmastide.

So this is a gift that can't be bought
A divine plan conceived beyond thought!
Look forward to sharing life above, eternally with a God of love,
Beyond the millennium!

Brian Fisher

Christmas

I love Christmas time
Because it cheers the barren wintertime
With love, joy and peace
When all men, women and children give and receive presents
And bring goodwill to their neighbours
Who lie peacefully by their side
Christmas trees, crackers and roast turkey
With loved ones who care
Carols which tell of a Saviour's birth
Who came to bring mankind new birth
Born in a manger in Bethlehem's fields
Because there was no room in the inn
Shepherds and wise men in nativity plays
And children who love to sing His praise
Snowmen, Christmas lights and mince pies to eat
Fun and laughter with friends to greet
But also we must remember the lonely and homeless
Who find Christmas a difficult time
When others are revelling, having parties
Who may never have known a loving home
Or have lost loved ones so dear and near
Let's pray for them that someone will share
The love of Jesus with them in word and deed
And make this Christmas special to them too
For Jesus came to save their souls as well.

David Cooke

Christmas Eve

The bleeping Tesco tills stand strangely silent
Each checkout girl has gone home to help Mum
With all of those last minute preparations
To make things perfect for the day to come
Baste the turkey, hang the decorations
Lace the bowl of punch with yet more rum.

Children's stockings hanging from the mantel
Pyjamas on by nine, well that's a first
Dad comes rolling in a little tipsy
Been out with the lads to slake his thirst
The church bells ringing in the distance
Remind us it's the eve of Christ's birth.

There's fairy lights adorning every window
Outside the freezing fog like crystal falls
Carol singers with their collars turned up
Are invited in to warm in welcome halls
Where red and silver banners boldly spell out
'A very merry Christmas to you all!'

John Morgan

Incarnation

An odd way of being born,
a stable on a winter's morn
but that's the way our Father chose
to send His Son among us.

If we'd been there, we'd not have known,
sin's deadly power was overthrown:
this baby was the Son of God
come down to live among us.

He came to teach us to be free;
he brought us life and liberty.
We saw his glory as he grew
and lived his life among us.

So look around this Christmastide
and see the others by your side.
Jesus lives in each of them.
He's still here among us.

Bernard Fyles

It Is That Time Of Year Again

We have reached that time of year again
Shops filled with Christmas cards
And thingy-me-bobs.

Shops filled with food
And thingy-me-bobs
You know the things I mean
Things you buy
And never use again.

It is that time of year again
Shops bursting with people
Pushing this way and that
All trying to get there
Before the last.

It is that time of year again
People have gone mad
Anyone would think they have never set foot
In a shop before.

While some poor soul
Has nowhere to go
Only a shop door
It's that time of year again.

Some are happy
Some are sad
While others are lonely
It is that time of year again.

Jane Coulston

It's Going To Be A Great Christmas, Don't You Agree?

I'm standing on the corner with a charity collection tin
Happy families throwing a few coins in
Smiling faces of little children looking forward to their Christmas
Their hopes and dreams and all that promises
Bright eyes beaming with imagination
Talking and planning with much expectation
I wish I was young again to feel the way that they do
Not only this Christmas but the whole year through.

Night air is getting colder; I decide to call it a day
Don't want to be late, want to see the nativity play!
Snow is falling heavier now as it sparkles and glitters
It's going to be a frosty night, along come the council gritters
Handing my collection tin to the lady at the gate
The nativity play hasn't started yet, luckily I'm not late
Sipping heavenly at my glass of warm mulled wine
Mmmm - that's when I know everything's going to be fine.

If asked what would make my Christmas dream come true?
I wouldn't hesitate and say all I want is you
I would love you to walk over to where I stand
Anticipating . . . with mistletoe in your hand
And when I see you making your way across the room to me
As I stand alone under the Christmas tree
I look down to your hand where the mistletoe lies
I catch my breath as I'm feeling quite shy.

But you're now smiling at me and you look into my eyes
I know right there and then that I'm in for a big surprise
Cos you're now holding the mistletoe directly over me
This is going to be a great Christmas, don't you agree?
Wow, this is going to be a great Christmas - for you and me.

Rita Bridgman

A Wish For You

The snow is falling gently now,
as I contemplate the passing of another year,
all that remembering does allow,
each smile and every tear,
yes, we've become a little older,
we know that time doesn't end,
but even though the nights are colder,
I hope we can still be its friend . . .

Friend to be more understanding,
with the strength of love to share,
wherever mankind is demanding,
to show that we really care,
the child is ours today
tomorrow a father or mother,
think of one that may . . .
be your sister of brother.

So the light fades beyond the brow
and the fire in the hearth dies,
the robin sings sweet on the bough,
as we say our last goodbyes,
I wish that this special night will,
always come round to bless
and all your memories fill . . .
you with peace and happiness.

Andrew Gruberski

Rock The Child

Rock the child, gently rock him
Mary so mild and so sweet
Hold him tightly, close to you
See not the nails in his feet.

Shepherds worship, adore him
You have left flocks drawing nigh
A lambkin as a gift, you're offering
See not the cross towering high.

Wise men, magi, come from the east
From far and distant lands
Guided by a bright star
See not the nails in his hands.

Yes, rock the child, gently rock him
Mary his mother so mild
God sent the earth His blessing
In Jesus, the Christmas child!

Babs Sherwin

Prayer And Peace

Christ be with us, as we pray,
Hope thou give, our people need
Remember us, Oh Lord today
Ireland here, a place of deed
Sorrow not, as you decreed
The time is right, let's break the shell
Many innocent slain and fell
Amid the tears, the grieving deep
Sons and daughters, mothers weep.

Love us all, just do our part
On us be peace, straight to our heart
Violent men, their deed to do
Enough we say, for me or you.

Pray this Christmas, peace be thine
Erin's shame, so black the name
Anguish felt, the tears that flow
Create in us, the power to show
Evil has, no love of us, it is our foe.

Prayer will help, of ones in need
Reflect upon, our holy deed
Ask and seek and you shall find
Your peace to come for all mankind
Earnest pleas to God on high
Regard God's love, for you or I.

Hugh Campbell

A Christmas Limerick

When Santa got stuck up the chimney,
His trousers just split at the seam.
Said Donner to Blitzen,
'We'll just have to fix 'em -
He's getting too broad in the beam!'

J M Gardener

Beside The Christmas Tree

I've left the seasoning of glad tidings,
Come from the secular side of me,
Submitting myself to humble thoughts
Beside the Christmas tree.

At this moment of serene quiet,
I reach deep into the thinking me.
Finding comfort in an aura-filled silence,
Beside the Christmas tree.

The lights are soft and mellow,
Their warmth reaches out to me.
As once again I hallow life's meaning,
Beside the Christmas tree.

Now others join in my serenity,
The family enriches the moment and for me,
My greatest gift, their love is here,
Beside the Christmas tree.

Comes the moment the lights seem brighter,
Laughter and joy abound around about me.
As the parcels of custom are gifted with that love,
Beside the Christmas tree.

Elwyn Johnson

My Kind Of Christmas

Dark December is coming
The streets are decorated with illuminations
With a flick of the switch, in the city
A warm festive glow is creating

My home in winter is so comfortable
With all the member's family
To go outside in the cold, I'm not able
Staying near the fire is so lovely

Having recollections of Christmas past
In my mind festive scenes within
With snow-sparkled branches of pine tree
A few balls and a golden star is topping

In church, in his crib baby Jesus is waiting
Everybody looks at Him adoringly
Celebrating the birth of the Saviour
Christmas carols we are singing

On the day of Christmas
Children are waiting impatiently
To open the nice presents
Chosen with love, carefully

Let Christmas be the season of peace
And goodwill to all men
A time of hope, love and best wishes
For all of you and my family.

Victorine Lejeune Stubbs

His Final Xmas (Card)

The envelope 'plopped' through the letterbox in the front room -
Onto the cold mat -
almost frozen because of the snow
He picked it up with a gloved hand,
'How nice of someone to be thinking of me at this time,'
. . . And so . . .
Read these words of the bard: 'A Merry Christmas' (it said)
'Just a line to let you know we're thinking of you at this time in
Agincourt' *signed by a black prince of long ago.*

Brushing dust off the mantelshelf, he placed it with the others
Eleven exactly the same

Then sat down - and wrote a 12th
in his name - on another white envelope - to send off -
there and then - in the lane

Wrote soothing words on the card
before placing inside the envelope's facade
Licked a stamp and went outside in the ice and snow
In The Midnight Hour to post it in the post box below
. . . Back to himself . . .
Wishing a good New Year: Better (He Hoped) than others up to press
Unaware he had been designated - only one more year left to go

Alan Knott

Vinegar

Something clattered down the chimney:
Christmas. It gave a wheezy gasp
and died right there on the hearth rug.
Sherry soused, with sooty beard askew,
unloosed teeth chasing grandkids around the room.

I'm in Hades with the roast potatoes
skidding in hissing lard like flambeéd dodgem cars.
A scattering of parsnips,
stuck in charcoal goo at the bottom of the pan,
like pale, julienned fingers pushing through the loose dirt
covering a damp cellar floor.
Gleaming steel knives grin down,
swaying on the rack above the rough, ensanguined chopping block.
The crackle of red wine spilling on the hob,
blood boiling on the coals.
Windows weeping condensation;
a lick of hair plastered to my forehead.
The Great Dictator,
at home in his kitchen.

This year I swear,
I'll skewer her to the nut roast with the carving knife
if she tells me the spuds taste like chips
and douses them in vinegar and not the jus that I prepared,
with Delia face down on the kitchen table.
Sticky, with her slip cover showing.

Vinegar? I'll pickle her sweetbreads
and keep them in the larder,
with the others.

Nicholas Proctor

The Travellers

When winter comes and the nights draw nigh,
And the frost glistens under a moonlit sky
The cold winds blow
And in turn bring snow
This then brings the travellers oh.

This happy group come each year
To perform their play and bring good cheer
Their clothes, their music
And merry laughter
Will touch our hearts for many days after.

The scene and action of their play
Takes you back to that first Christmas Day
How a babe was born
On Christmas morn
And Herod, of course, was put to scorn.

It's not hard to guess that these folk believe
In everything they say and they truly leave
You in no doubt
What life is all about
And the villagers say these folk are really devout.

The travellers soon will leave this place
And of this group you'll find no trace
Except a sense
Of reverence
That lingers with some awesome suspense.

We love to see these travelling folk
For 'tis they that bring sincerity and hope
We wish them well
Where next they dwell
As we wait with expectation for the next *Noel!*

Maureen Alexander

Innocence By The Firelight

Cracking, the sapling underfoot
as each branch breaking.
Burnt out embers within
a fiery tomb siphons our oxygen.
Where the smoke will go
and the candles blow, out there.
There is the empty plastic stocking,
waiting for the Botox gift from Gran.

But, the snow slips silently
silencing the buds of spring -
as the downtown church remembers the King of Kings.
His swaddled self amongst the sheep,
quietly snoozing with the snow, as he sleeps,
so whilst the wings of snow-angels
amuse us for the eve,
the beckoning warmth, of fireside slumber
calls we saints into the purifying glow.

Lozi Bolton

Changes

The Christmas tree appears tattered and old
The baubles have lost their sheen of gold
Decorations neglected and forlorn
Blooded wreath for those who mourn.

Glitter and sparkle in an ash heap lay
Eerie shadows cloud, Heaven's brightest day
Trumpets sound, the King of Kings is born
But a blooded wreath for those who mourn.

A lamented robin, against a vacant sky
Watches trees, flowers, the Earth die
Magic's lustre is cracked and torn
Blooded wreath for those who mourn.

E Christie

Christmas

A pile of lovely presents heaped beneath the Christmas tree,
All tied with tinsel ribbon for everyone to see;
A hundred toy bells ringing on the boughs with utmost glee.
Such a joyful, happy time is Christmas!

Even though the ground is covered with a blanket of white snow
And icicles are glinting in the gentle moonlight glow;
The warm inside is waiting for every friend and foe.
Such a friendly cosy time is Christmas!

Roast turkey in the oven, hot roast potatoes too,
A gorgeous pile of hot mince pies, delicious, crisp and new,
And to look for threepenny pieces in the pud is what we do.
Such a lovely time for food is Christmas!

Throughout this joyous feasting, with its warm and friendly glow,
We dine and sing so merrily and sparkling wines do flow,
But I sometimes find me wondering how many of us know
The real and truest meaning of Christmas.

It's really held in memory of our Lord's birth long ago,
When He came from God in Heaven to this poor Earth below;
And so to church on Christmas morn each one of us should go
To thank the Lord for such a time as Christmas.

I enjoy exchanging presents and the games that we all play,
But I love to hear the church bells proclaiming Christmas Day,
Remembering to thank the Lord for sharing His birthday.
Such a blessed, holy time is Christmas!

Margaret Worsley

Alternative Christmas

From love she let him go, not sponsored by survival,
For Christmas; he would leave and no revival.
How was she to know there was something in the air
Incredibly, emerged an endurance course so unfair.
The spirit of it a tangle of his thoughtless mind
No consideration of a cash-strapped wife left behind
Knowing it to be right, the lack of emotion chilling
A moment of truth to link a plot unwilling.
His busy year left her devastated
It became clear when all in vain she waited.
Never an informed decision, consequently ending,
No alternative to being dropped was pending
Life seemed so cold, but he didn't seem to know
Yet asking nothing, when from love, for Christmas, she let him go.

Betty Bukall

Christmas Fun

Christmas is finally here
It brings joy and it brings tears
Lots of presents big and small
Plenty of gifts for one and all.

People playing in the snow
Boys and girls with bright red nose
Snowball fights - a lot of fun
Happiness for everyone.

I am sad when Christmas ends
It's so much fun
I wish it could be early next year!

Georgia Forsyth (8)

A Lonely Christmas

Some people at Christmas
So very sad and alone
No friends or families
Where gifts are shown
No tree, no chatter
Alone they are
To bring blessings
Of the beautiful star
To be lonely away from all
Just a card, a call
No Christmas dinner
For some to taste
Just memories to relate
No cosy fire to sit around
Christmas, love and companion is found
The chatter of children
May be far away
A prayer, a thought
That is all it takes
To ease those
Who are sad and heartbreak.

Maureen Thornton

My Christmas Prayer

Our Father of every race
Make all life, commonplace
We give our life to every Heaven
Share food and drink and all our land
So black-and-white can hold each hand
Hurt not your neighbour, make him a friend
Commit no murder but love we send
Promise forgiveness and not revenge
Keep us from evil temptations and hate
So we can enter Heaven's Gate.

Dugald McIntosh Thompson

A Sad Note At Christmas

This year will be sad
Said a mother to her lad
Daddy has left for another world
Will not be glad at the Christmas herald.

Listen to your mother, son now
And try to echo hope on show -
So we can raise a cheer for Dad
The way we did before so glad.

We will listen to the church bells
Once again ringing for Christmas, tell -
Of the God who came for men
But sadness fills us now again.

Susannah Woodland

Carols On Milk Street

On Milk Street with frozen hands
Ears red-tipped
And noses that dripped
We sang.
Songs of good cheer
Of this pure time of year
Songs the missus asked to hear.
And warm mince pies of melting bliss
No cold caroller could resist
Kind onslaught of neighbours Christmas wish.

Then, 'We wish you a merry Christmas'
And with breath-clouded faces
And snow's soft embraces
Went singing on our way.
Our pockets a-jingle with pennies from Heaven,
Carolling on Milk Street
This Christmas Eve day.

Miki Byrne

Christmas Eve

The carol singers have gone leaving their footsteps in the snow
The Christmas tree looks radiant with fairy lights aglow
Christmas presents and decorations sparkle in the firelight
Mince pies and sausage rolls are baked, they look a tempting sight
The children were so excited as they tiptoed up to bed
Each carrying their stocking and thoughts of Santa in their head
The clock has just chimed midnight, snow is falling thick and fast
I sit down for a moment and think of Christmases past
I think of people on their own at this time of year
And of unfortunate needy children living so far and near
I say a prayer for peace in the world, hoping love will find a way
As our Lord Jesus Christ was born on Christmas Day.

Hazell Dennison

Forward Press Information

We hope you have enjoyed reading this book - and that you will continue to enjoy it in the coming years.

If you like reading and writing poetry drop us a line, or give us a call, and we'll send you a free information pack.

Alternatively if you would like to order further copies of this book or any of our other titles, then please give us a call or log onto our website at www.forwardpress.co.uk

Forward Press Ltd. Information
Remus House
Coltsfoot Drive
Peterborough
PE2 9JX

(01733) 898101